DRAW LIKE AN

A SELF-PORTRAIT SKETCHBOOK

Patricia Geis

Princeton Architectural Press · New York

Long before
cell-phone cameras existed,
artists created self-portraits.
The first self-portrait that we know of dates
back to the year 1300 BC in Egypt. This was
something rather unusual back then because, for centuries,
only the very powerful could be portrayed. What's more,
the ancient Egyptians didn't even have mirrors to see their
reflections in! Artists usually make self-portraits
by looking at themselves in a mirror, although
sometimes they make portraits using their imagination,
their memories of themselves, or of their emotions.
Every artist creates their self-portrait
in their own style.

are you ready
to create your own !

Portrait of Giovanni Arnolfini and his Wife, Jan van Eyck, 1434
Oil on oak, 32 ¹¹/₃₂ x 23 ⁵/₈ in. (82.2 x 60.0 cm)
National Gallery, London

VAN EYCK

At the beginning of the fifteenth century, many people couldn't afford to have mirrors in their homes, and weren't used to seeing their own reflections. (Can you imagine that?) But during the middle of the century, mirrors were affordable to anyone. Artists began using them to become a part of the artistic process not just as spectators but also as figures within the work. So they began poking themselves into the works they created. This example by Jan van Eyck might be the first self-portrait of an artist within a painting. Where is the artist? Can you see where he is reflected?

Draw yourself as if you were the artist of this painting. How would you see yourself?

4

Self-portrait, Albrecht Dürer, 1498
Oil on panel, 20 ^{15}/$_{32}$ x 16 ^{1}/$_{8}$ in. (52.0 x 41.0 cm)
Prado Museum, Madrid

DÜRER

Albrecht Dürer portrayed himself as the subject of some of his paintings to proclaim that painters were creators and not mere artisans subject to the whims of a client. Here he painted himself as he wished others to see him—as an artist and a gentleman, elegant and refined.

How would you like for others to see you? Create an elegant self-portrait showing how distinguished you are, for you're a real artist!

Self-portrait with beret, wide-eyed, Rembrandt Harmensz van Rijn, 1630
Etching and burin, 1 $^{31}/_{32}$ x 1 $^3/_4$ in. (5.0 x 4.5 cm)
Rijksmusem, Amsterdam

REMBRANDT

When we're happy, surprised, sad, or frightened, we are still ourselves. Rembrandt Harmensz van Rijn captured his own image at specific moments, adding an expression of confusion or surprise, through drawings done as swiftly as the click of a camera.

Draw yourself expressing an emotion. Do it quickly, before it disappears!

The Artist in His Studio, James McNeill Whistler, 1865–66
Oil on paper mounted on panel, 24 ¾ x 18 ¼ in. (62.9 x 46.4 cm)
Art Institute of Chicago

WHISTLER

In this painting, James McNeill Whistler captures a moment from his daily life. He shows himself in his studio surrounded by his muses; one of them is dressed in a kimono and holds a Japanese fan in her hands. He is surrounded by his things, his furniture, his collection of Chinese porcelain. He looks at us as if we had suddenly stumbled onto the scene, interrupting his work. In representing his surroundings, he is also defining himself.

Draw yourself and what surrounds you. Where are you? Who are you with?
What do the things around you say about you?

Self-Portrait with a Straw Hat, Vincent van Gogh, 1887
Oil on canvas, 16 x 12 ½ in. (40.6 x 31.8 cm)
Metropolitan Museum of Art, New York
Legacy of Miss Adelaide Milton de Groot

VAN GOGH

Artists often use self-portraits to experiment with and perfect artistic techniques, since the model is always available. In this painting, Vincent van Gogh did just that, using only lines of color to paint himself.

Look carefully at how Van Gogh uses the strokes of colors to shape his face.
Paint your own self-portrait in the same style, using only the colors yellow,
green, red, dark blue, light blue, and white.

Self-Portrait in Two Dimensions, Kazimir Malevich, 1915
Oil on canvas, 31 ½ x 24 ⅜ in. (80.0 x 62.0 cm)
Stedelijk Museum, Amsterdam

MALEVICH

Kazimir Malevich believed that artists must understand what they see, think about what they saw, and then portray it on the canvas using shapes and a totally new artistic language.

Look at yourself in the mirror, meditate on what you see, and create a self-portrait using geometric shapes. Reimagine yourself using the figures from pages 41 and 42.

My Portrait, Tamara de Lempicka, 1929
Oil on wood, 13 ²⁵/₃₂ x 10 ⅝ in. (35.0 x 27.0 cm)
Private collection

DE LEMPICKA

Self-portraits are not only graphic expression but also a way for artists to present their ideas. In this self-portrait from 1929, the artist Tamara de Lempicka appears as a woman who is assured, modern, and independent, at a time when women were very often expected to be the opposite.

Paint your own self-portrait in a green Bugatti! Make your face look assured and confident, as if saying, "I'm behind the driver's wheel, I'm in control!"

Self-Portrait, Piet Mondrian, 1942
Pen, ink, charcoal, and gouache on paper, 24 ½ x 18 in. (62.2 x 45.7 cm)
Dallas Museum of Art, Foundation for the Arts Collection
Gift of the James H. and Lillian Clark Foundation

MONDRIAN

Piet Mondrian thought that it wasn't always necessary to represent textures, surfaces, curves, shadows, or even colors. Everything should be simplified, eliminating the unnecessary. According to him only straight lines, vertical and horizontal, were necessary to draw the most basic and important aspects of things.

Make your own self-portrait in the style of Mondrian, simplifying your features until only what is essential remains.

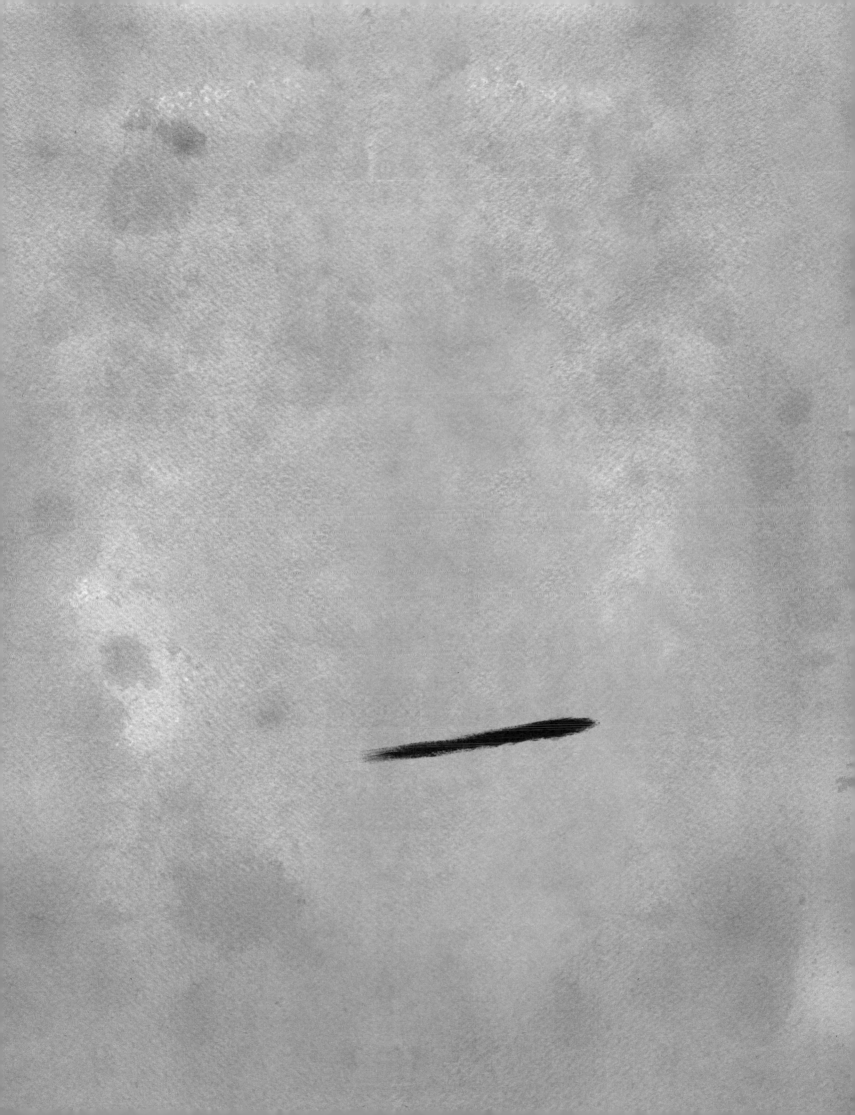

Self-Portrait with Monkeys, Frida Kahlo, 1943
Oil on canvas, 32 $\frac{3}{32}$ x 24 $\frac{25}{32}$ in. (81.5 x 63.0 cm)
The Jacques and Natasha Gelman Collection

FRIDA KAHLO

The people and animals we love are a part of our lives. In this painting, Frida Kahlo is surrounded by four monkeys, who represent the four students she taught at the time and who called themselves "Los Fridos." Kahlo adored animals and always had many exotic creatures in her home. In portraying her students as her beloved little monkeys, she revealed her affection for them.

How would you represent the people and animals you adore in your self-portrait?

Self-Portrait, Maurice Miot (Melito), 1948
Lithograph, 25 $^3/_{16}$ x 19 $^{11}/_{16}$ in. (64.0 x 50.0 cm)
Private collection

MAURICE MIOT

When we look in the mirror, we see ourselves from the outside. But what about from within? Maurice Miot, known as "Melito," wanted to express the parts of us that aren't visible—all the ideas bouncing around inside our heads!

How would you portray your thoughts and ideas? With colors? With words? With drawings? Draw an outline of yourself in black, then color it in with whatever passes through your mind.

Self-Portrait, Pablo Picasso, 1955
Ink on cardboard, 15 ⅝ x 12 ½ in. (39.7 x 31.8 cm)
Private collection

PICASSO

Pablo Picasso thought that whether facing forward, in profile, with his back to the viewer, looking to one side, or with his mouth open or shut, he was still Pablo Picasso. That's why he wanted to represent all of those positions at the same time in one image.

Pay close attention to this self-portrait: the head is turned to the right, the nose points to the left, one eye looks straight ahead, and the other is in profile. Make your own Cubist portrait, mixing your features in different angles and positions!

Self-Portrait in Profile, Marcel Duchamp, 1958
Colored paper on a black background, 5 ⅝ x 4 ²⁹/₃₂ in. (14.3 x 12.5 cm)
Private collection

DUCHAMP

A shadow is the simplest and most exact portrait. Marcel Duchamp created a template of his profile, cut out 137 colored silhouettes, and then glued them each onto a black base and numbered them. The inscription on the base, "Marcel dechiravit," means "Marcel tore this quickly."

Place yourself in profile between a lamp and a wall and ask someone to trace your shadow on the sheet of paper on page 43. Cut it out by hand, very carefully. (Marcel tore his quickly because he had lots of practice.) Remove what would be your face and stick the remaining part on the right-hand page.

26

The Son of Man, René Magritte, 1964
Oil on canvas, 45 $^{21}/_{32}$ x 35 $^{1}/_{32}$ in. (116.0 x 89.0 cm)
Private collection

MAGRITTE

René Magritte thought that appearances were deceiving. Sometimes people want others to see them in one way, but their real nature is another. In this self-portrait, Magritte conceals his face behind an apple.

Where would you draw yourself? Would you place yourself, as Magritte does, behind the apple? Would you place yourself beside it, or in front of it? Make your own self-portrait with the apple, and place yourself wherever you want!

Self-Portrait II, Jean Dubuffet, 1966
Marker on paper, 9 27/32 x 6 ½ in. (25.0 x 16.5 cm)
Fondation Dubuffet Collection, Paris

DUBUFFET

Jean Dubuffet thought that art was found where one would least expect it. An artist didn't need to study, nor apply all the rules taught in art academies. According to Dubuffet, pure art is that which arises spontaneously.

Draw your self-portrait while thinking of something else, freely, without analyzing, like the doodles you make when you're distracted. Start by drawing your face, beginning at point one and ending at point two, without lifting your pen from the page. Then, color it in however you want. Automatically, without thinking!

WELCOME BACK TO YOUR PUBLIC LIBRARY

The "public" is now free to handle this book.

Take a moment to think about what that means.

• • •

Wash your hands

consider quarantining your book for a few days, open it up and enjoy reading!

.1

.2

Self-Portrait, Roy Lichtenstein, 1976
Oil and magna on canvas, 42 x 36 in. (106.7 x 91.4 cm)
Private collection

LICHTENSTEIN

Why do we make portraits of ourselves at rest when we are so often in motion? In order to create a sense of dynamism, Roy Lichtenstein made this self-portrait with slight changes in position, like a blurred photo. He was a Pop artist who used the language of comic strips in his work: black outlines; bright primary colors; and the dots and stripes used to print comics, but enlarged greatly.

Make your own version of a self-portrait in movement. Draw yourself in four slightly different positions, using a different color for each: black, red, yellow, and blue.

Untitled (1960), Jean-Michel Basquiat, 1983
Acrylic, charcoal on paper over board, 36 $\frac{1}{32}$ x 24 in. (91.5 x 61.0 cm)
Enrico Navarra Gallery, Paris

BASQUIAT

In the 1970s, graffiti artists would leave their signatures, or "tags," in the subways and on the streets of New York City. Over time they added drawings, phrases, and even self-portraits. They painted as a form of protest and, above all, to leave their mark on a society that didn't take them into account at all. Jean-Michel Basquiat began creating graffiti with a friend, using the tag SAMO, but soon his artwork—spontaneous, colorful, and rebellious—left the streets behind to be exhibited in the most exclusive galleries and museums.

Paint a self-portrait in a graffiti style and sign it with your own tag so that the whole world will know that you created it!

34

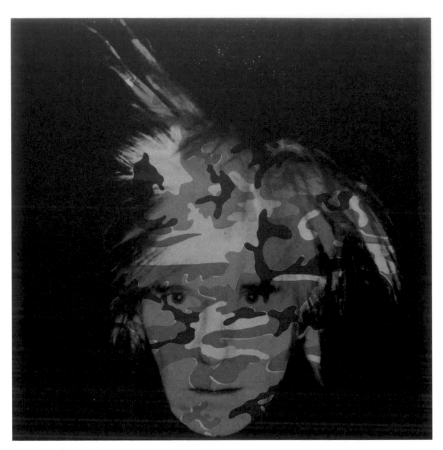

Self-Portrait, Andy Warhol, 1986
Acrylic and silkscreen on canvas, 80 x 80 in. (203.2 x 203.2 cm)
Metropolitan Museum of Art, New York

WARHOL

Andy Warhol knew the importance of the image and was the first artist who used his own image to promote himself. He made hundreds of self-portraits with eccentric styles so that everyone would know that he was the most modern and most popular artist of his time.

Make your own self-portrait to create a name for yourself as an avant-garde artist!
Cut out the sheet on page 45 and use it to print out or photocopy a black-and-white photograph of your face. Don't forget to pose with a really expressive look! Then glue it onto the page at the right.

Self-Portrait, Vik Muniz, 2003
Collage, 100 x 72 in. (254.0 x 182.9 cm)
Private collection

MUNIZ

Every day we are surrounded by images of people—on television and in newspapers or magazines. To make his self-portrait, Vik Muniz cut out pieces from portraits he found in magazines.

Draw the outline of your face and your features in pencil, then cover them with a mosaic made from little bits of the portraits you can find on pages 47 and 48. You can use large or small pieces, as you prefer; if you're really patient, you can cut the pieces out using a hole punch!

EXTRA MATERIAL

42

FLASH

Issue 22

FASHION SPECIAL

WINTER IN THE CITY

SAFARI

Issue 303

EXTRA

The RUINS OF
TIBI
THE PERUVIAN AMAZON
FROM PUCALLPA TO IQUITOS